Success of Hispanic Magazine
by: John Garcia

The Success of Hispanic Magazine traces the history of Hispanic Magazine and specifically the staff members and their job descriptions. Jr. high students and older may find this book inspirational as far as a specific cultural group is concerned and informative as it explains the production of a magazine. However the two are intertwined and since the staff are introduced with their own personal history, the book may not remain timely, or be conveniently used as a reference for how to publish a magazine. -- Reviewed by Jill Martin

THE SUCCESS OF

Hispanic Magazine
A PUBLISHING SUCCESS STORY

JOHN GARCÍA

Photographs by Ricardo Vargas

WALKER AND COMPANY

NEW YORK

First published in the United States of America in 1996 by Walker
Publishing Company, Inc.

Published simultaneously in Canada by Thomas Allen & Son Canada,
Limited, Markham, Ontario

Library of Congress Cataloging-in-Publication Data
García, John A.
The success of *Hispanic* magazine: a publishing success story /
John García; photographs by Ricardo Vargas.
p.   cm.—(Success series)
Includes bibliographical references and index.
Summary: Describes the people and processes involved in the
production of *Hispanic,* a popular magazine which focuses primarily
on positive news related to all aspects of Hispanic American
culture.
ISBN 0-8027-8309-0 (hardcover).—ISBN 0-8027-8310-4 (reinforced)
1. Hispanic.   2. Hispanic American periodicals—Juvenile
literature.   [1. Hispanic.   2. Hispanic Americans—Periodicals.
3. Periodicals, Publishing of.]   I. Title.   II. Series.
PN4900.H57G37   1996
051′.08968073—dc20   95-38612
CIP
AC

Printed in the United States of America

2   4   6   8   10   9   7   5   3   1

Contents

Juanita Torres greets visitors as they arrive at Hispanic.

· 1 ·

A Vision for a People

People are almost always tense when they have to meet with their bosses about work. *Hispanic* magazine executive editor Robert Macias feels that way when publisher Alfredo Estrada calls him into the office to discuss a story idea Alfredo had proposed and Robert had changed. Most of the time this tension between the two helps to create an exciting, vibrant magazine.

On Tuesday, January 10, 1995, the new year began for the *Hispanic* magazine senior staff with an informal meeting to go over a recently delivered story. Alfredo Estrada, Robert Macias, and managing editor Melanie Cole got together after each had read the article separately. The story, tentatively titled "Latinos on the Info Superhighway," dealt with the new boom in using computers to send information over the phone wires. *Hispanic* magazine's owners were exploring the idea of developing an on-line publication, making the story as much a resource for *Hispanic* as for their readers.

Alfredo, who had suggested the story, called the staff in to the unscheduled meeting to discuss their views. He agreed to eliminate a sidebar (a small part of the story), and that another sidebar needed more focus. And he wanted to eliminate some of the repeated information. Then the staff turned to the main story. It was not written the way Alfredo had originally imagined it. "I wanted to see more specifics in the story, I wanted more resources mentioned, and I wanted more focus," recalls Alfredo. Fortunately

Some of the staff meet to discuss the new issue: (left to right) Carlos Manzano, Alberto Insúa, Barbara Fernandez, Alfredo Estrada, Romeo Perez, Linda Ramirez.

for the staff, they all agreed with his criticisms of the generally well-written article.

Robert Macias and Melanie Cole had joined *Hispanic* just six months earlier, soon after the magazine moved to Austin, Texas, from Washington, D.C. "I think we're jelling as a staff," says Alfredo. "We were all on the

MAGAZINES ARE OLD

Webster's Dictionary defines a magazine as "a periodical containing a collection of articles, stories and pictures, or other features." Usually bound inside a paper cover, the typical magazine specializes in one particular subject area, such as sports, world news, or Hispanics. Philadelphia philosopher, inventor, and publisher Benjamin Franklin and a rival, Andrew Bradford, are each credited with publishing America's first magazine in 1741. Franklin's publication, magnificently titled *The General Magazine, and Historical Chronicle, for All the British Plantations in America,* was planned before but not published until three days after Bradford's *American Magazine, or A Monthly View of the Political State of the British Colonies* appeared. Both magazines targeted an educated, cultured class of people, many of whom were familiar with this new type of publication, for they were already popular in England. Magazines quickly became attractive to the expanding American population, and by 1888, more than 3,500 magazines were published in this country.

Today there are more than 70,000 magazines in the United States. The endless choices include magazines for dance music aficionados *(Hip Hop),* airline pilots *(Pilot),* jazz musicians and fans *(Down Beat),* African-Americans *(Essence),* computer buffs *(PC Magazine),* and those interested in news and popular culture *(Newsweek).* Almost 100 magazines are dedicated to travel alone.

The history of magazines geared to Latinos in the United States is sketchy. One of the earliest magazines was *El Habanero (The Havanian).* First published in 1824 in Philadelphia and New York, *El Habanero* was also the first Spanish Catholic magazine published in the United States. Its publisher, the Reverend Felix Varela, was a philosopher and professor who was born in Cuba. *El Habanero* was one of the first newsmagazines published in this country. It often carried stories about politics, science, literature, sports, religion, and other subjects.

same page with the story. This story will do a good job of educating readers about the potential of the information superhighway."

Educating readers about Hispanic culture is the underlying mission of the Hispanic Publishing Corporation, creator of the 250,000-circulation monthly magazine *Hispanic*. Be they Hispanic or non-Hispanic, readers around the country get a healthy dose each month of positive news, features, and analysis about Hispanics in politics, sports, and fashion.

"We have a fairly broad audience of people who are really involved in their communities," says Alfredo Estrada. "We created this magazine to answer the call from many Hispanics who wanted a publication that portrayed them honestly. They wanted a national magazine that told them success stories about Mexican-Americans in the Southwest, Cubans in Miami, and Puerto Ricans in New York. We're never at a loss for stories."

Most of *Hispanic* magazine's senior staff is itself a microcosm of the United States' different Hispanic groups. Alfredo Estrada and Robert Macias are Cuban. Associate publisher Carlos Manzano is Puerto Rican, community relations director Randy Belcher-Torres is Mexican-Indian, and art director Alberto Insúa is Peruvian. Marketing director Tony Barajas, marketing manager Linda Ramirez, advertising director Romeo Perez, associate art director Derrick Caballero, and assistant editor Valerie Menard are Mexican-American. Circulation director Gary Meo is Italian, and managing editor Melanie Cole's family comes from Kansas by way of Europe.

Hispanic staff members like to think they offer a special service to a special group of people. Described by the publisher as a "cross between a Hispanic *People* and *Time*," *Hispanic* has an upbeat, lifestyle- and feature-dominated editorial content. It is an English-language publication targeted to the fastest-growing minority group in the country. A 1990 U.S. Census report estimated that by the year 2025, Hispanics will outnumber African-Americans and become the largest minority group in the United States.

Hispanic is designed to be a consumer magazine. Consumer magazines—the widely read *People* magazine is one of the most popular—offer their readers stories about all aspects of life from sports, education, and en-

HISPANIC®

MARCH 1995

Features

28
Whose Vote
Is It, Anyway?
How the religious right fights for
the Hispanic vote.
By Ines Pinto Alicea

16
Interior Instincts
The design world embraces the
work of Vicente Wolf.
By Darcy De Leon

22
COVER
Women on the
Verge . . .
Four brash Latina writers
transform the literary landscape.
By Jennifer Mena

36
CARS
Pick Up the Pace
In 1995, trucks move beyond utility
to fun and luxury.
By Valerie Menard

50
Culture
Comforts
How Hispanic organizations help
college students build a home away
from home.
By Eunice Moscoso

58
SPECIAL REPORT
Exploring the
Internet
Why Hispanics need to get on the
Information Superhighway.
By Derly Andre Tijerina

Departments

2

COVER PHOTO BY DANIEL CIMA

Hispanic *(March 1995)*

tertainment to politics, health, and national news. *Hispanic* magazine publishes stories about all these subject areas but concentrates on the Hispanic people involved in them or on how these issues touch Hispanic lives.

For many people of Hispanic descent, the magazine does much more than just publish stories about their culture: It helps correct misconceptions. *Hispanic* magazine stands out in a publishing environment where Hispanics are not fairly portrayed in the media. Many Hispanics complain that the print media write stories about them only when they are involved in crime or have low scores in school. Alfredo Estrada says loudly and clearly that his magazine's aim is to portray the positive. There is limited space for negative news. "When you look at mainstream publications," says Alfredo, "you get a negative, slanted portrayal of Hispanics. *Hispanic* magazine's job is to present the opposite of that view."

The Hispanic media have always had an important role in exposing Americans to the cultural heritage of Hispanics. National publications such as *Hispanic Business* and *Hispanic Link Weekly Report,* newspapers like New York's *El Diario-La Prensa* and Los Angeles's *La Opinion,* and the TV networks Univision and Telemundo have operated for years and are well respected by Hispanic and non-Hispanic readers and viewers. By the mid-1980s, the nation's two largest organizations for Latino journalists, the National Association of Hispanic Journalists and the California Chicano News Media Association, each grew to almost 1,000 members. In addition, Latino journalists have formed local news media associations around the country. These groups work to improve the image of Latinos and promote the hiring and advancement of Latinos in the news media. It was in this atmosphere that *Hispanic*'s parent was born.

Two of the most highly respected role models for young Hispanic reporters today are Arturo Villar and Harry Caicedo. Each has been a writer, reporter, editor, and publisher for close to thirty years for various publications, and each has helped create and support Hispanic media groups. Back in 1984, they announced plans to launch a national consumer newspaper insert dedicated to Hispanic culture: *Vista*. "We had tried a similar kind of publication in Latin America and we knew it would work," explains Arturo,

HISPANIC MAGAZINES

Name	Circulation	Frequency	Editorial focus
Hispanic	250,000 (paid, 40,000)	Monthly	An English-language magazine for Hispanic professionals, highlighting Hispanics' achievements.
Ser Padres	330,000 (paid, 7,000)	Bimonthly	A Spanish-language magazine distributed in doctors' offices and hospitals. Focuses on infant care, family life, and family concerns.
Vanidades	86,485 (paid, 64,308)	Biweekly	A Spanish-language women's magazine focusing on food, fashion, and beauty.
Vista	1,074,951 (paid, 0)	Monthly	A bilingual publication distributed in newspapers. Focuses on entertainment and business personalities.

now the publisher of *Latin America Business Reports*. "There was nothing like this in the United States. Nobody was targeting U.S. Hispanics in a general circulation publication."

Because most of the growth in the Hispanic population over the previous ten years had come from new immigration, the founders of *Vista* had to decide whether English or Spanish was the better language to reach Hispanics. "There was confusion, and there still is, over what is the better language," says Fred Estrada, Alfredo's father and chairman of the Hispanic Publishing Corporation. A marketing study told *Vista*'s creators and investors, including Fred Estrada, that English was the better choice. *Vista* magazine still prospers as a bilingual national consumer newspaper insert now run by the Hispanic Publishing Corporation.

Fred Estrada, an engineer by trade, was struck by the success of *Vista* magazine and the reception the magazine received. "I noticed the immediate impact we had on Hispanic issues," he says from his Miami office. He and Alfredo began to think about starting a national consumer magazine patterned after *Vista*.

Alfredo Estrada points to a specific publishing event that helped crystallize his father's decision to publish a national magazine. "I remember the *Time* magazine cover in 1985 that proclaimed the 1980s as 'The Decade of Hispanics,'" he recalls. The story profiled Hispanic empowerment, the community's growing population and political clout, and the art, dance, literature, and music characteristic of Hispanic culture.

In the summer of 1987, Fred Estrada, Alfredo Estrada, former New Mexico governor Jerry Apodaca, and some other family members launched *Hispanic* magazine. The initial 50,000-circulation preview issue was given free of charge to influential Hispanics around the country, mostly educators, business leaders, and community-based Hispanic organizations. The magazine was an immediate hit. Many people had never seen an English-language magazine that featured Hispanics.

By April 1988, the magazine was launched as a regular 150,000-circulation monthly. The issue of that date featured a photo of Venezuelan actress Raquel Welch on the cover. The immediate, positive response from subscribers and advertisers surprised the publishers. "The smartest thing we did was to promote the publication as a national community magazine," remembers *Hispanic* community relations director Randy Belcher-Torres.

This Month

Racing for a Dream

With a vision and drive that have turned his dreams into reality, Ralph A. Sanchez, president and founder of Miami Motorsports, Inc., has reshaped the face of motorsports in South Florida.

Thirteen years ago, the long-time real estate developer and investor brought auto racing to South Florida when he founded Miami Motorsports, Inc. and staged the East Coast's first street racing event in downtown Miami. Although a downpour cut short the inaugural race of the Miami Grand Prix in 1983, the

Racing promoter Ralph Sanchez (inset) is the driving force in bringing a permanent IndyCar facility to South Florida.

race established a motorsports tradition here which has had a growing economic and cultural impact on South Florida.

On March 4 and 5, the Marlboro Grand Prix of Miami, presented by Toyota, will feature the season opener of the 1995 PPG Indy Car World Series, the most-watched American motorsports series in the world. Miami Motorsports has a long-term agreement to bring the season opener to Dade County. Sanchez describes the upcoming race as the "single biggest event" in the company's thirteen-year history. As host of the season opener, Miami stands to attract a television audience of more than 400 million people in more than 110 countries worldwide. Some of the best-known names in the sport—Emerson Fittipaldi, 1994 Indianapolis 500 winner Al Unser, Jr., Adrian Fernandez of Mexico, and Raul Boesel of Brazil—are slated to compete in the Miami race. Sanchez says the 1995 race is attracting the largest influx of teams, sponsors, members of the press, and fans in the history of South Florida racing.

With the completion of the Homestead Motorsports Complex,

Hispanic Almanac

March 21, 1806 is the birthday of Mexican statesman Benito Juárez. Born of indigenous parents, he was a key figure in the overthrow of the dictator Santa Anna in 1855, led the liberals to victory in the War of the Reform, and served as president in 1858–62 and 1867–72. During his tenure, Mexico prevented France from establishing an empire in Mexico and saw a transfer of political power from the *criollos* to the *mestizos*. Juárez's birthday is a Mexican national holiday.

a permanent racing facility in South Florida to be managed by Sanchez, the promoter is making a high-octane run at elevating auto racing to one of South Florida's premier attractions.

Cine en Español

Chicagoans are in for a treat this month when Chicago Latino Cinema, sponsored in part by Columbia College, presents its eleventh annual Chicago Latino Film Festival—recent feature films, shorts, and videos from Latin America, Spain, Portugal, and the U.S. On Friday, March 24, the viewing begins at the Art Institute of Chicago, with one of the most popular films of Colombian cinema, *La Estrategia del Caracol* (*The Strategy of the Snail*).

This year's festival honors three great, recently departed actors: Spain's Fernando Rey, Argentina's Hugo Soto, and Puerto Rico's Raul Julia. Comedies, dramas, documentaries, animated features, and experimental programs will be shown at several venues, and directors, actors, and film executives

One of the festival's feature films, produced and directed by Fernando Sariñana.

will lead post-screening discussions. All films are in their original language with English subtitles. Tickets are $4 to $6; festival passes $50 to $80. For more information, call (312) 431-1330.

Hispanic *(March 1995)*

"The last couple of years we have not changed our direction; we just expanded on what has worked." The magazine turned a profit in its third year and is never at a loss to fill advertising space.

Despite its reader acceptance, media watchers have complained that *Hispanic* magazine's credibility suffers because it publishes too many "good news" stories. One said, "There are too many important problems in our community, and they [*Hispanic* magazine] always concentrate on the good." But Mercedes Oliveras, a journalism professor at Texas Christian University, believes *Hispanic* magazine has its mission firmly in hand. Positive news about the Hispanic community is sorely needed, she says, and *Hispanic* magazine should be applauded for its work. "It's a great image builder for Hispanics and for the Hispanic media," says this journalist, who has written extensively about Hispanics and the media in her eighteen years as a columnist for the *Dallas Morning News.* On the other hand, she also agrees with some of the complaints about the magazine: "Stories in general are not as substantive as they should be. They are not . . . into hard news, and our community needs hard news reporting."

Alfredo Estrada believes the focus of the magazine has changed in the last several years—from a concentration on lifestyles to a harder, more serious, sometimes controversial editorial mission. During 1994, for example, *Hispanic* published stories on the difficulty of being gay in the Hispanic culture ("Coming Out, Standing Out," June), environmental racism ("Green Injustice: Who's Winning the Race for Environmental Dollars," November), and a political insiders look at the problems of the congressional Hispanic Caucus ("The Hispanic Caucus: United or Divided?" September).

"We've done some hard-hitting journalism here," says Alfredo. "I don't think we can be accused of being only a soft news publication when we put Linda Chavez on the cover [in August 1992]." In that issue was a profile of the controversial author and top-level official under former president Ronald Reagan. Chavez was also a leader of the English-only movement, which some considered an anti-Hispanic cause. The cover story generated more than 100 letters to the editor. The staff was thrilled—people were talking about *Hispanic* magazine! Some readers cheered the magazine for profiling an intelligent, successful woman. Others were angry at the magazine for giving publicity to someone who they felt had insulted Hispanics. It was the type of response Alfredo Estrada had dreamed about.

Hispanic*'s new office building.*

· 2 ·

The Publisher Publishes

The creative energy of *Hispanic* magazine is nurtured in a brightly lit, organized office in Austin, a city whose strong Spanish heritage makes it a fitting home for the country's premiere Hispanic magazine. The tiny reception area announces to visitors that here is a hip, successful business; its walls are covered with numerous awards from design, business, and political groups and several examples of contemporary Latino art from Peru, Mexico, Argentina, and other Spanish cultures.

With an open door that mirrors his managerial style, Alfredo Estrada's office is sparsely furnished with only a desk, table, a leather chair for the publisher, and two simple chairs for visitors. No fancy posters or pieces of art clutter this office—seemingly the quietest of *Hispanic*'s many small work areas.

With the phone and intercom regularly interrupting discussions, Alfredo seems to have mastered the art of speaking to several people at once. The room is always filled with staff members talking about plans, studying pictures or graphics, or just chatting.

This day he is talking to me, the author, about the "Latinos on the Info Superhighway" story. Like many people today, he is comfortable with computers and understands their potential. This story was his idea, and he wants to make it work his way. "I want this story to be a resource for people," says Alfredo. "People are confused about the information highway, and I want to cut through the fog. I want phone numbers; I want help; I want specifics."

Alfredo's job is to be a "jack of all trades." At many large magazines, the publisher's sole role is to supervise sales and advertising promotion, working closely with corporate leaders to persuade them to advertise. Many publishers are former sales executives who leave the production and editing of their magazines to others. But on many smaller magazines, such as *Hispanic*, the publisher is more closely involved in all aspects of the publication, from advertising to editing. Most of these publishers trace their backgrounds to the writing and editing end of the business. Alfredo Estrada, a former lawyer, had little professional experience as a writer and reporter when he came to *Hispanic* magazine. But like many lawyers, he has a respect for clear writing.

"At many small magazines it is common for the same person to have the

Alfredo is involved in many aspects of Hispanic. *Here, he and art director Alberto Insúa make a design decision.*

ALFREDO ESTRADA

Hispanic magazine publisher Alfredo Estrada believes that the best way to manage a staff with diverse duties and assorted needs is to treat them the same: with an open-door style and with fairness. "We're small enough that I can get involved in many things and listen to many people," says Alfredo, a thirty-seven-year-old with no formal management training but instinctive leadership skills. "I think I learn well from my mistakes, and in this business you make them."

Alfredo Estrada and his father, Fred, began planning *Hispanic* magazine soon after Alfredo graduated from Georgetown Law School in 1984. The younger Estrada worked as a corporate lawyer in New York for three years before moving to Washington, D.C., to begin the magazine. Though he was familiar with publishing through his involvement with a similar publication, *Vista*, he had never run a new company before.

"It was difficult putting together a whole brand-new organization," remembers Alfredo. "You have to deal with personnel issues—get staff, people you can trust. *Hispanic* was a complete startup company. I got a lot of guidance from a lot of people."

For the past seven years Alfredo has dedicated himself to Hispanic Publishing Corporation, which he runs with his father. Every month, the company publishes more than one million issues of various magazines, including *Hispanic* and *Vista*.

"The challenge for any manager is to get people motivated," notes Alfredo. Another difficult challenge, he says, is to get your staff to see your vision. "I need people to translate my vision for the company into a publication. It's easy to get people to do what you say, but it's harder to get them to believe in what you're saying."

THE STORY BUDGET

A story budget is a list of stories to be published by a magazine or newspaper. A story budget is usually produced during the month in order to let the staff know what everyone is working on and where stories are coming from.

The budget is created over several weeks of story meetings between the publisher and the editorial staff. These stories get listed on the budget according to their importance and the available space for editorial pieces in the publication.

Hispanic magazine's story budget for the March 1995 issue listed the following information for each story: type of article, length, working title, and author.

Cover

Features   Pg.

Latina Writers

Political Issue	(4)	"The Religious Right and Hispanics" (Ines Pinto Alicea)
Profile	(2)	"Vincente Wolf, Interior Designer" (Darcy de Leon)
Miscellaneous	(4)	"Trucks" (Valerie Menaud)
Business/Tech	(5)	"Latinos on the Info Highway" (Derly Andre Tijerina) Sidebars: "LatinoNet" (Federico Cura), "Getting Started" (Laxman Gani), "Day in the Life of an Internet User" (Michael Chorost)

Special	(6)	"*Hispanic* on Campus" 2-page feature: "Hispanic Student Groups" (Eunice Moscoso); 1-page career col: "How to Write a Résumé" (Maris Reyes); "Cornell Protest Update" (Ines Pinto Alicea); "BLIPS": soccer scholarships, Trinity premed students, Puerto Rican Jr. College. Factoid: Schools with Highest Hispanic Enrollmentt
Departments		
Business	(1)	"Low-Doc Loans" (Irene Thomas)
Executive Travel	(1)	"Book on Tapes"; "Destination: Des Moines"; "Product Box: 7-11 Phone Card"
Travel	(1)	"Buenos Aires" (Federico Cura)
Money	(1)	"Retirement Planning: Act Now to Minimize 1994 Taxes" (Justo Martinez); "Consumer Tip: Federal Brochures—Avoiding Fraud"
Career	(2)	"New Mexico Career Event" (Alfredo Estrada)
Health/fitness	(1)	"HIV-Positive Mother, HIV-Negative Child"; "Sport Parent" Book
La Buena Vida	(2)	RCA Small Dish, Facconable Men's Perfume, Sony Sports Walkman, Oscar de la Renta, Charity Scarves, Puerto Rican Hot Sauces
Hispanic Agenda	(1)	Illegal Immigration
Reviews	(2)	Books: *Spidertown, El Teatro Campesino, Face of an Angel* Music: Emilio Navaira (John Ramirez); Misc Latin (Mark Holston)
Forum	(1)	"What My Culture Means to Me" (Darlene Gallardo)

Stock		
Table of Contents/	(3)	
From the Editor/		
Letters		
This Month	(4)	"Spotlight": Events; Carnaval/Calle Ocho in Miami; Latino Film Festival. "Hispanic Almanac": TK; "Coast to Coast": Graig Rivera of *Inside Edition* (Guy Arseneau); NY-Playwright Edwin Sanchez (Gary Stern); AZ-Border Health and Environmental Network (Tim Vanderpool); CN-Borenquin Dance Theatre (Cheryl Becker); National-Chavez Fights Illiteracy (Eunice Moscoso); CA-Wrestling Champ (M. Sanchez); Pocho cartoon.
Calender	(4)	

roles of editor and publisher," says Alfredo. "As publisher I want to promote the magazine. In terms of stories, I tend to get more involved in the career, business, and now technology issues."

This smart-looking and smart-talking 37-year-old complains about the unfair portrayal of Hispanics in the general media and praises other minority publications and businesses that debunk those stereotypes. The Hispanic Publishing Corporation, which publishes *Hispanic* magazine, is headed by Alfredo's father, Fred, but Alfredo Estrada has free rein in running the magazine. "This is a total departure from practicing law," he says. "Publishing is a difficult business, and you have to be very committed to the long hours. There is a lot of pressure not to make mistakes."

But Alfredo hasn't made many mistakes since he started the magazine with his father in 1988. As publisher, he frequently speaks to business and college groups and others interested in Hispanic culture. He is often interviewed by newspapers and TV reporters about Hispanic media issues. He is particularly busy promoting the magazine around Cinco de Mayo ("Fifth of

May," the Mexican Independence Day) and Hispanic Heritage Month in the fall. "I'll make sales calls if need be; I don't mind," says Alfredo, an unpretentious man who speaks his mind. "I'll do whatever has to be done to make this thing work."

As noted earlier, Alfredo took a special interest in the "Latinos on the Info Superhighway" story, which was his idea. It appeared on *Hispanic*'s story budget (a list of stories to be published) in December of 1994. Before its publication in the March 1995 issue, it would travel through a maze of editing, design, layout, and production people, pass through a printer 1,000 miles away from the home office, and land in the hands of almost 250,000 people courtesy of U.S. postal workers and shippers around the country. Several thousand people would buy the magazine at newsstands or pick it up at a local school or Hispanic organization.

In the following chapters we'll take a closer look at the various steps in the publication process.

Valerie Menard's desk shows that there's a lot going on in the editorial offices.

· 3 ·

Writing and Editing

Through the selection of stories, editors give a publication its soul and identity. Famous magazine editors in chief such as Helen Gurley Brown of *Cosmopolitan* and Henry Luce of *Time* assigned and edited stories that reflected their interests and personality. The images of *Cosmopolitan* as a sexy, hip, successful publication and *Time* as an informed, contemporary magazine were created through the pesonalities of those editors. It is often said that editors are the people who make publishers' dreams about their publications come true. It is through the process of assigning, writing, and editing stories that the editorial content of a publication comes to life.

An editor is often viewed as someone whose sole job is to make weak writing better. But many publications employ editors whose duties are varied. Publisher Alfredo Estrada acts as *Hispanic* magazine's editor in chief, a role that can be likened to the manager of the publication team. As editor, he guides the course of the magazine's editorial and art departments: He decides which stories will be published in upcoming issues and approves final design ideas and layouts.

Though the ideas for stories may come from other staff members and writers outside the staff, it is the editor's job to select stories that fit in with the publication's tone and editorial direction. The "Latinos on the Info Superhighway" story was first proposed by Alfredo, and he deemed it important enough to be a feature article. "This story and this issue fit in perfectly with our idea of being a publication that reaches out to everyone, not just one type of Hispanic group," he says.

ROBERT MACIAS

"My greatest fear is boredom," says *Hispanic* magazine executive editor Robert Macias. Robert has turned this fear into a philosophy. At the age of thirty-one, he has held almost every position in magazine editorial work, from writer to copy editor to proofreader and even computer system designer and supervisor.

After graduating from the University of Texas at Austin in 1986 with a degree in English, he embarked on his goal of writing the Great American Novel. "I was a waiter during college and I liked it, but it just seemed that with a degree I should be doing something else."

Needing to make money in order to be able to write, he took what he thought would be a temporary job as a copy editor at a home and garden magazine in Houston. The magazine took on a more gritty tone, which Robert liked, and he ended up staying two years. "You learn very quickly about a subject once you get immersed in it," says Robert about the gardening aspects of the job. He didn't start the novel, but during this time he did write the Great American Romantic Screenplay.

After having been placed in charge of the computer system at the gardening magazine, Robert found that he was not getting any of his personal writing done, so for six months he joined a friend in a video production company. But that job also didn't allow him time to write. Next he took a job managing special sections for the *Houston Post,* where he worked for a year. By this time his screenplay was making the rounds in Los

Angeles and he was getting calls. "L.A. people tell me they are still interested, but who knows," he says.

There were other freelance writing and copyediting jobs and a part-time job as a proofreader at the *Houston Chronicle,* but by 1993 Robert was hungry for some stability. *Hispanic* magazine came to town in 1994, and he landed the job of executive editor.

"I don't regret the leaps of faith or the risks I've taken because in many ways they have prepared me for this job," says Robert. "Despite the ups and downs of my career, I don't want to be a burnout case. I always look for challenges."

Hispanic's executive editor, Robert Macias, supervises all of the editorial staff, as well as the freelance writers, copy editors, proofreaders, and fact checkers. He is also involved with the art department. Managing editor Melanie Cole oversees more of the day-to-day operation of the editorial department. Robert, Melanie, and assistant editor Valerie Menard all keep a watchful eye on the progress of every writing assignment. A typical issue of *Hispanic* contains at least thirty stories, ranging from a 2,000-word cover story to smaller features and several letters to the editor.

An editor must be intellectually curious, be able to spot trends early on, and have a wide range of general knowledge. Because Robert Macias is familiar with computers, he had some strong opinions about "Latinos on the Info Superhighway." "I knew that I wanted to make it less of a political story and more of a people story," he recalls. He talks in a measured, exacting voice. "I wanted the story to be a call to action. Something that would get people excited about the possibilities of the information superhighway."

Robert didn't have to search far for a writer. Most magazines employ freelance writers to create their stories. These writers are not on the payroll of the magazine but work for many different publications. Melanie Cole had worked with the writer Derly Andre Tijerina at a computer magazine called *Cadence.* Robert knew his work too. He contacted Derly six weeks before

Melanie, Valerie, and Robert discuss the latest version of a story.

"Latinos on the Info Superhighway" was due. Derly immediately accepted the assignment. The two men agreed on what kind of story would be written and on Derly's fee.

A writer can spend months becoming an expert on a given subject, interviewing many people in order to present different opinions on an issue or issues. By becoming an expert, the writer hopes to communicate the nature of the subject and the characters in the story. Derly's familiarity with computers allowed him to write most of the story from memory, yet he still spent hours reading documents, records, and previously published stories on the same subject. Research can be a tiring process, but it is also very satisfying. Derly says he learned much from his research.

"The process of writing is always enlightening," reports Derly, a forty-

FINDING WRITERS

Many times a writer interested in publishing a piece in *Hispanic* sends executive editor Robert Macias or managing editor Melanie Cole a query, a short outline of the story with a list of people to be interviewed and themes to be covered. If Robert likes the story idea, he negotiates a salary with the writer and assigns a due date. Sometimes, staff members come up with the ideas and write the story themselves. Robert, Melanie, and assistant editor Valerie Menard are frequent contributors to the magazine. Alfredo Estrada writes a monthly publisher's column, and art director Alberto Insúa has contributed pictures. Other times the story is assigned to one of *Hispanic*'s regular freelance writers or to a newcomer selected by Robert.

Recognizing that it is hard for Hispanics to break into journalism, Robert tries to use as many Hispanic writers as possible. Studies show that though Hispanics make up 9.3 percent of the U.S. population, Hispanic employment at newspapers stands at only 2.6 percent. Magazines have an even worse record for hiring Hispanics. "I feel that one of my duties is to encourage Hispanic writers and so I always try to hire them," says Robert, who had a successful freelance career before joining *Hispanic*. But he also recognizes that it would be impossible to limit all the writing in the magazine to Hispanics: ". . . I have to get the best writer for the magazine and the specific assignment." Being Hispanic is *not* a requirement for working at the magazine.

Hispanic is the editorial home to an impressive group of writers that includes former *Chicago Tribune* editorial writer Manual Galvan, former surgeon general Dr. Antonia Novello, and the *Wall Street Journal* business writer Julie Lopez. The magazine pays its writers a fee comparable to that paid by other magazines with the same circulation: approximately $800 for a 2,000-word story. Every month, the magazine receives hundreds of queries, a sign that it has gained a level of respect throughout the freelance market.

Robert Macias had an easy time as-signing the information superhighway story.

year-old who is a technical consultant as well as a writer. He majored in business at Fairleigh Dickinson University in New Jersey but also took several writing courses there. He says he was comfortable with the revisions to the article made by Robert Macias. "I understand that a piece must fit a style of a magazine. I don't let anyone change facts, but I know they [*Hispanic*'s staff] have to shuffle things around to make this story consistent with the whole magazine."

Derly sent the completed story to *Hispanic* magazine on a computer disk, which simplified the editing process. "Latinos on the Info Superhighway" was loaded into the office computer, where it was stored as a master version. Robert Macias, Melanie Cole, and Valerie Menard then took turns reading the one version and entering comments into the computer. This master version became the working copy from which all the editing was done.

Because of his extensive editing staff and the endless assignments, Robert Macias, like most executive editors, does very little editing of the actual words. He mostly looks through a story to ensure that the writer followed the agreed-upon direction of the piece. He also makes sure that Hispanics are quoted in the story and that all sides of the issues are represented. Many times, if there are major changes or corrections to be made, Robert might consult with the writer on rewriting the piece.

In most cases, "the editing can be done without a rewrite," he said. But the story still needed an introduction. As Robert explains, "newspaper writers write short stories so they get to the point quickly. In magazine writing, we like long stories with introductions."

The trio of *Hispanic* editors have divided up much of the editorial work. One editor is chosen to supervise a main feature one month, while another

Melanie Cole's editing helps the reporter's story fit the goals of the magazine.

EXPLORING THE INTERNET

Why Hispanics Need to Get on the Information Superhighway

BY DERLY ANDRE TIJERINA

These days, you can't go any-where without hearing talk about the Information Super-highway. Government and big business tout its potential, the high-tech community pounces on every new idea it produces, and yet millions of average Americans who plugged in their new computers after Christmas couldn't even find the on-ramp to this mythical place. It is difficult to get a true perspective on what it all means. And the Hispanic community faces a daunt-ing task: to not only gain access to the Internet but to do it *now*, at a time when the social and political dimensions of technological change are being measured in imaginary numbers.

What is this so called Information Superhighway? It is a metaphor for a series of digital networks linked togeth-er, called the Internet. Simply put, a net-work is a system with two or more points in at least two distinct physical locations that are linked together by a common mechanism to move something back and forth. By this definition, the highway system, the telephone system, and the postal service are all networks. The Internet enables users to move information, as opposed to cars or mail, from one point to another.

The concept of a network becomes more complex when discussing the Information Superhighway, however, because it deals with abstract ideas that are not yet fully defined. Users of all nations and back-grounds face similar challenges as they learn to explore and comprehend the informational landscapes available on the highway. Amidst the slick jargon, it is important to see the Internet as a net-work of individuals and organizations designed to exchange information.

It's impossible to predict the eventual numbers of users and organizations and the amount of information that will be involved. Regardless of the final size of the infrastructure, the four basic compo-nents on this information network remain: the user or information consumer, the elec-tronic access device or desktop hard-ware, the information the user wishes to access, and the technical wizardry and operating software which, for lack of a better word, I call the "magic."

As we consider the information com-ponent, we must enlarge our under-standing of what "information" really is. At its most basic, information is a mechanism used to package and trans-fer data and ideas independent of its form. With mature digital technology, the information on the superhighway takes all kinds of forms—numbers in a bank account, textual documents such as let-ters, audio files for voice mail or music, even compound documents that include text, music, and full-motion video.

The display device is the next neces-

58   ILLUSTRATIONS BY CHARLES BEYL

will edit other parts of the magazine. Robert Macias and Melanie Cole frequently handle the features, and Valerie Menard is responsible for several departments, such as travel, health, and money. Robert was the lead editor on the "Latinos on the Info Superhighway" story, but Melanie read it first.

"I could see that it had some ideas that you could hang a story on," recalls Melanie. But she felt it didn't have the right feel for a magazine story. "It had too much explanation and not enough story line, but he [Derly Andre Tijerina] came up with several great ideas and conclusions."

Editors sometimes look for dramatic words or phrases they can develop into leads (the first two or three sentences of the article that capture a reader's attention) and openings (the beginning that tells what the story is about). Derly Andre Tijerina's story focused on who would control the *magic* of the on-line world. Robert Macias and Melanie Cole loved the use of that word and used it throughout the story.

Once the final version of the story was approved, Melanie and Valerie copyedited for spelling, grammar, and sentence structure. A copy editor trims words and phrases to make the writing more powerful, clear, and concise, without changing the writer's style or meaning. A good copy editor acts as the guardian of language for his or her publication. A copy editor at a sports magazine, for example, must know the difference between American football (the game where you run and throw the ball) and European football (the one where you kick the ball and which is called soccer in this country). The copy editor also makes sure a story does not contain any language that could be seen as offensive to any group of people. Many copy editors study English, journalism, or writing in college. Some get added experience working on college newspapers or yearbooks.

"You have to really care about language to be a good copy editor," notes Melanie Cole. "Anyone interested in this field should start out with their school newspaper or literary journal. And read, read, read."

Copy editors are faceless workers in the world of publishing. Their names never appear on a story, but they almost always play a major part in making the piece come alive. A good, experienced copy editor at a major magazine or newspaper can expect to be paid almost $40,000 a year, and such editors are always in demand. *Hispanic* magazine also uses copy editors

MELANIE COLE

Hispanic magazine managing editor Melanie Cole doesn't see editing as dry and dull. There is always a place to have fun and be productive. Several years ago while editing a "very dry, academic" journal she hit upon a trick she still uses.

"I try to read the copy backward or with a funny voice," she says with a laugh. Reading a story in such a manner makes you concentrate on just the words and not the meaning, she says. "After I've read it several times for meaning, sometimes it's hard to check it for spelling and grammar, and so I read it backward."

Melanie's career as a teacher, writer, and editor has moved forward since she graduated from the University of Kansas at Lawrence. She taught college-level freshman English, then moved to Texas to pursue a doctorate. Her first editing job was at the scholarly journal where she picked up her backward reading trick.

For a while Melanie edited a Texas state employee retirement newsletter. She also worked for a banking firm and computer magazine as a copy editor and newsletter publisher. Then she got a dream job at the prestigious *Texas Monthly,* a magazine known for its excellent writing. She started out as a copy editor and in five years was named associate editor. She joined *Hispanic* in 1994.

At *Hispanic,* thirty-seven-year-old Melanie supervises the day-to-day editorial operation of the magazine. She frequently acts as editorial traffic cop by pushing stories through the editing system, making sure they move from step to step. She usually takes charge of one or two feature stories every month, assigning the writer and supervising the story and copyediting once the story is turned in.

Except for the backward reading, a trick she says, "[that] is not something I tell everyone about. I do it in the privacy of my own home," most of her time is spent making sure copy is moving smoothly.

PROOFREADERS' MARKS

The symbols below are used by copy editors and proofreaders to indicate changes and corrections in copy.

lc Lowercase letter
c capitalize letter
ital Set in italic type
lf Set in lightface type
bf Set in boldface type
tr Transpose letters
tr Transpose words the in line
⌐ Move right
⌐ Move left
⌒ Close up
Leave some space

⊙ Insert period ⊙
ʌ Insert comma ʌ
⊙ Insert colon
ʌ Insert semicolon
ʋ Insert quotation marks ʋ
Sp Spell out
⊥ Use one-em dash
¶ Begin a paragraph
run in Run in or run on
ℒ Delete and close up
e/ Add a letter ʌ

31

Valerie's copyediting goes unnoticed by the average reader, but it's crucial to keeping Hispanic's reputation as a high-quality magazine.

who are interns—college students who work at a publication for credit or work experience. The publication follows the editing style of the Associated Press, a national news service that has set guidelines for word, sentence, and grammar usage.

After a story is copyedited, Valerie Menard checks it for accuracy: names are checked for proper spelling; job titles are confirmed; any inconsistencies regarding time or dates are corrected. Robert, Melanie, and Valerie all check the final version. Publisher Alfredo Estrada then gets a chance to review the story and make any changes he feels are necessary—but by this time the changes should be minor. He gets to see the story again once those changes have been made.

By this point, the story has been completely reviewed by a *Hispanic* magazine staff member almost ten times, including three times by Robert Macias and three times by Alfredo Estrada. This process is followed for all of the three to five major pieces published in the magazine every month. The stories are now ready to be turned over to art director Alberto Insúa, who has been working on other elements of the issue for almost a month.

In the 1990s, art departments are filled with computers.

· 4 ·

The Art Director and the Image

On most magazines, the art director controls the appearance of the entire publication. This is an important responsibility because many advertisers and readers base their support on how a magazine or newspaper looks. The serious financial publication *Forbes*, for instance, would not hire an art director who has a reputation for funky and funny designs since those designs wouldn't match *Forbes*'s image.

In their choice of type, color, and illustrations, art directors give their publication an identity that matches the editorial content. But every art director will say that making the pages attractive and appealing is secondary to making them more readable.

For example, the first job Alberto Insúa tackled once he joined *Hispanic* was to redesign the publication's logo—the magazine title as it appears on the front of the magazine and elsewhere. The logo is the company trademark. Choosing the right logo is important because it must set the magazine apart from other publications in a crowded newsstand. It must attract attention and create a suitable mood. Most of all, it must help sell magazines. "The old logo looked old-fashioned and hard to read," says Alberto about the blocky type used in the first several issues of *Hispanic*. "I wanted something clean, contemporary, and long lasting." He chose Futura typeface for the magazine's name—a typeface he says is "not a fad type."

His job also requires assigning artwork to freelancers and supervis-

HISPANIC

MARCH 1995 $3.00

Write On!

Latinas Shake Up
The Literary World

Novelist Julia Alvarez

SPECIAL REPORT

EXPLORING THE INTERNET

Hispanic *(March 1995)*

ing their performance. He tends to hire photographers and illustrators— most of whom design on computers—who are "fresh and like to experiment." The thirty-four-year-old accomplished artist spends hours poring over design books that feature the work of various artists. He also spends time meeting with prospective artists and photographers who want to work for *Hispanic*. These freelancers can be paid from $200 to $800 for a cover photograph or full-color illustration, depending on their experience and the difficulty of the assignment. *Hispanic* magazine often features computer-generated and hand-painted illustrations on the front cover.

"It's very important that you set the proper tone for your magazine right from the front cover," says Alberto. He notes that a magazine with a young audience, such as *Rolling Stone*, can be more experimental in its design. "Our readers are young, but we target older people too so our design might be a bit more conservative than *Rolling Stone*'s."

Art directors come from varied backgrounds. Some have studied as photographers, illustrators, artists, or production managers. They must be experts in *typography* (use of typefaces), layout, illustration, and the use of paper. Though many art directors have attended first-rate design programs such as those at the Parsons School of Design in New York City or the Art Center College of Design in Pasadena, California, it is not necessary to attend one of these schools. Any college with a good graphic design program should offer enough basic training for this field. An entry-level job as an assistant or designer, where you might get to design infographics or headlines, should be the next step. But no matter where they get their training, art directors are often some of the highest-paid employees at a publication.

Hispanic's art department can be considered a state-of-the-art electronic design studio. It is backed by powerful computers, several color monitors, advanced illustration and photo-editing software, and removable hard disks. Alberto Insúa's department completes most of the page designs and all of the layouts electronically. Most of the stories include at least one *infographic*—a computer-generated chart, graph, or map that helps readers quickly absorb information related to the story.

ALBERTO INSÚA

When art director Alberto Insúa walked through the door of *Hispanic* within months of the magazine's start, he found out he had been hired to create a department. "There was no art department," he remembers, half-smiling. "I didn't even have a table. No supplies, no computer, nothing." No problem.

He would produce the magazine several times using the "old-fashioned" method. He constructed the pages by pasting the text and photos on cardboard with glue. But this didn't slow him down. He would soon redesign the logo, choose new typefaces for the magazine, and begin to build an art department. Now he works in a state-of-the-art design studio with computers, scanners, and optic drives.

"It's changed just a bit," he says sarcastically. "Electronic makeup allows us to experiment much more than in pasteup. I can see the color changes on the screen instead of building a page in black and white."

Alberto became interested in art and design while a boy in Lima, Peru. During his childhood he enjoyed drawing but preferred to go surfing. Seeking to get more serious training in painting and design, he moved to the United States and began to study, first at Montgomery College in Maryland, then at the prestigious and challenging Corcoran School of Art in Washington, D.C.

While working for an advertising agency as an assistant art director, he applied for and was offered the *Hispanic* magazine job. He looked at the position as an opportunity to help create a magazine's image and immediately accepted the job.

"We've done much in the way of building the image of this magazine," he says proudly. The magazine is very up-to-date. "You never want to be old-fashioned or cliché. You want [*Hispanic*'s] readers to think that you're as hip as they are."

Assisted by associate art director Derrick Caballero, Alberto experiments on the computer with the layouts for different pages. The text is sent electronically from the editing department to the art department's computers. The page-layout program stores the design elements, such as the various sizes and colors of type. The program then automatically converts the editorial copy to the styles established for the magazine by Alberto. Headlines, bylines (the name of the writer) and captions (text under a photograph or other illustration) can be put in place in minutes. Illustrations and pictures are captured by the computer through a scanner and placed in their spots on the screen page.

This process of completing the page layouts on computer is called *pagination.* It is a relatively new technique that saves thousands of working hours and dollars. Yet designing all the different elements of a publication is still a big job. The "Information Superhighway" issue, for example, involved a cover illustration, several other major illustrations, plus almost fifty other photos, about 21,000 words of text, and more than fifty ads.

"You have to create a unity, a continuity throughout your publication," says Alberto. "The whole package must come together like it makes complete sense."

COMPUTER INFOGRAPHICS

Computers now allow designers to provide information with greater visual impact. Computer-generated graphics give readers information in a variety of ways: through words, photos, charts, maps, or diagrams. These *infographics* enable designers to present complicated material in an easy-to-digest form. Infographics address readers' complaints that pages full of words are dull. The graphics make the information more attractive to the eye. Writers can also leave more complicated information out of their story, making it easier to read.

Infographics can take the form of boxes with short biographies of featured characters, sidebars of a timeline, graphed statistics, a chronological table, or a list of events.

The art of putting together these infographic elements in a magazine has become a growing field. Graphic designers now have to act as reporters in order to analyze the material being presented, at the same time coming up with innovative ideas on how to present it.

Here's an example of an infographic detailing the production schedule for "Latinos on the Info Superhighway," which appeared in the March 1995 issue of *Hispanic* magazine:

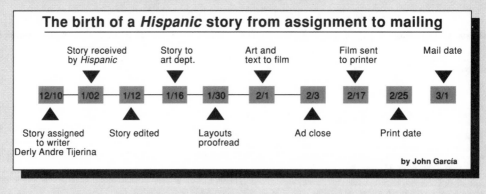

The birth of a *Hispanic* story from assignment to mailing

Story received by *Hispanic*	Story to art dept.	Art and text to film	Film sent to printer	Mail date

12/10 — 1/02 — 1/12 — 1/16 — 1/30 — 2/1 — 2/3 — 2/17 — 2/25 — 3/1

Story assigned to writer Derly Andre Tijerina — Story edited — Layouts proofread — Ad close — Print date

by John García

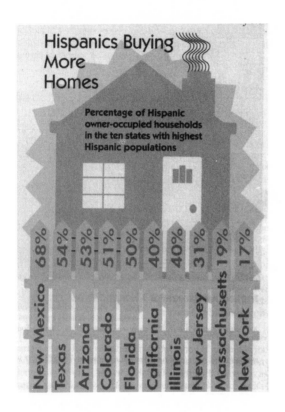

One of many infographics used in Hispanic.

For the most part, *Hispanic* magazine is a very reader-friendly publication. Boxes, arrows, graphics, and photographs all come together to make readable pages. The typography, photographs, and other illustrations all seem comfortably at home on Alberto Insúa's pages.

Derrick Caballero supervises the production of Hispanic, *both from his desk and on press when the magazine is printed.*

· 5 ·

Finally a Print

After months of producing text and illustrations, all the work is turned over to the production manager, who supervises the production cycle. This might be the most crucial assignment in the production of the magazine. Weeks of fine-tuning color photos and illustrations on the computer can be for nothing if the proper ink is not used or the printing press is not capable of reproducing the original artwork.

Though most magazines employ a full-time production manager, *Hispanic* entrusts this important assignment to the art department, mostly associate art director Derrick Caballero. "The most important thing in production work is keeping the issue on schedule," says Derrick, a designer for twelve years.

Hispanic magazine's production is completely computerized. After all the stories, ads, headlines, photos, and other illustrations are entered into a computer and art director Alberto Insúa completes his layout, he saves all his work on a computer disk. Alberto takes the computer disk to a separation house, a company that produces the film and proofs of the issue.

The page proofs are sheets of paper that provide full-color reproductions of each page and ad. These proofs are shown to every editorial staff member as well as to art director Alberto Insúa. Everyone carefully checks them for mistakes. A page proof might go back and forth to the separation house several times before everything is approved for printing. Derrick Caballero keeps a detailed account of who reviews the page proofs, whether they find mistakes, and whether the mistakes are corrected. After all the editing the

Derrick and Romeo Perez (national advertising director) talk about the proofs of the ads in the latest issue.

pages have gone through to this point, the staff is happy to find only minor mistakes.

Each page is then printed out as film. The color pages are separated into four pieces of film, each of which shows only one of the four basic color groups: black, magenta, yellow, and blue. These colors combine to produce all the colors needed to produce a full-color photograph. These films are then sent directly to the printer in South Daytona, Florida.

Almost every month, Derrick Caballero or Alberto Insúa travels to South Daytona to supervise the press run. Soon after the films are delivered to *Hispanic*'s printer, R. R. Donnelley & Sons, they are converted to printing plates. These plates are inked with their respective colors, and then each is passed over the paper, producing a blend of colors that duplicates the original art or photographs.

"When we go to Daytona, we're there to check that the color we envisioned in the design is the color that is coming out of the press," says Derrick. "I go over each page [in the press run] to make sure all the colors fit together."

The press used to produce *Hispanic* magazine can print 150,000 copies of an entire eighty-page magazine, in four colors, in under five hours. Each sheet of the coated paper that comes off the press contains thirty-two pages of *Hispanic* magazine. The pages are folded, trimmed, and collated, then stapled along the spine. *Hispanic* provides the mailing labels, and the issues are shipped directly from the plant.

As marketing manager, Linda Ramirez helps publicize Hispanic *to potential readers.*

· 6 ·

Advertising, Marketing, and Public Relations

A publisher may know writing, editing, and design, but if he or she doesn't know advertising, marketing, and public relations, the publication will never serve its audience. At *Hispanic*, marketing director Tony Barajas, advertising director Romeo Perez, marketing manager Linda Ramirez, and director of community relations Randy Belcher-Torres work closely with associate publisher Carlos Manzano to boost income, promote readership, and develop programs that generate interest in the magazine.

The importance of advertising sales varies from magazine to magazine. *Reader's Digest* gets about 70 percent of its revenue from subscriptions, 22 percent from advertising, and 8 percent from newsstand sales. But *Hispanic* magazine is a controlled-circulation publication, which means it is given to selected readers for free. Because these readers don't pay for the magazine, almost 95 percent of *Hispanic*'s income comes from advertising. Thus the advertising and marketing departments of the publication are very important.

A certified public accountant by training, Carlos Manzano has the role of supervising all financial action at the magazine. His office is bigger than the one occupied by his boss, evidence of the importance placed on keeping track of the company's sales. Around his desk are wall-mounted charts detailing every ad sale from the past eighteen months, broken down by month and category. Carlos is able to look at one of these charts and quickly assess if his magazine made money during a particular month. He's able to tell if enough companies from one sector of business, such as computer or car vendors, have bought ads during the past month or year. The charts sometimes tell him he might have to make a pitch to one of his colleagues.

"I have to go into Romeo's office and say, 'Please sell some more ads,' " Carlos says with a laugh. He is sitting at his desk at 8 A.M., having already scanned a computer list of ad sales for the month. "Our ad department supports this magazine from month to month. This is a very easy business to spend money in, so I have to strike a balance between what I spend and what I get from ads and subscriptions." He watches sales to avoid having to go into Alfredo Estrada's office with bad news.

Advertising director Romeo Perez supervises nine advertising representatives in Detroit, Washington, D.C., Los Angeles, Chicago, and New York. Many of these advertising representatives work for a number of magazines—a common practice in publishing. It is Romeo's job to make sure that every section of the United States is covered by a sales representative.

Carlos Manzano's walls show that he has all of Hispanic's *financial data at his fingertips.*

CARLOS MANZANO

How does a Puerto Rican with little English language skills graduate from the University of Maryland, land a job at the biggest brokerage house in the country, then become the controller of a large publishing company?

"Persistence boarding on obsession," says *Hispanic* magazine's associate publisher, thirty-two-year-old Carlos Manzano. Carlos moved from his native Puerto Rico to Maryland at the age of twenty with a strong cultural identity and the urge to study finance and business. He juggled work at Merrill Lynch and studies at the University of Maryland.

"I would read books with a dictionary right next to me," he remembers not so fondly. This trial-and-error system did little for his school grades but did help him learn a valuable lesson: "School taught me that there really are no limits if you're persistent. It taught me that you can only be defeated if you quit."

After graduating with a degree in finance and business, Carlos studied for his certified public accountant exam at nights. He joined *Hispanic* magazine in February 1988, two months before the publication came out with its first issue. He served as controller, then became the associate publisher in charge of the publication's finances.

Carlos deals with all the advertising and financial affairs of the magazine. He watches the rate of advertising and uses the expected sales and income from subscriptions and newsstand sales to map out a budget for the month. Higher sales mean more income, maybe a bit more expenditures on stories or art and maybe more pages.

"I track the money," he says with a gleam in his eye. "It's what I always wanted to do."

Carlos, Derrick, and Romeo meet to discuss ad sales for the month.

"Every day I get a report from these people that informs me about sales or plans," explains Romeo. He makes frequent visits to each territory. "These people know the territory they're working in, so I just go around to make sure things are running smoothly."

Romeo was happy to find out about the "Latinos and the Info Superhighway" story. "People see these kinds of cutting-edge stories in our magazine, and they get the sense that we're relevant and current. Current with a Hispanic twist," he says, adding that technology stories sell well with regular *Hispanic* clients such as IBM and other computer companies.

Sales representatives call on clients armed with many tools to promote the magazine. One indispensable tool is *Hispanic*'s rate card, a breakdown of advertising prices based on the size of the ad. Evidence of advertising successes, such as letters from satisfied customers, favorable reprints of arti-

Romeo Perez takes his time in hiring experienced, well-organized sales reps.

cles about the magazine, and, of course, copies of the magazine itself are other useful sales tools.

Because of advertising's importance to the financial survival of a publication, positions in ad sales departments offer the best potential for making a high income in publishing. According to a magazine industry survey, a successful ad sales person at a major consumer magazine can expect to earn a yearly income of close to $100,000 in a percentage of sales and salary. Advertising sales directors can top $150,000. At many magazines, like *Hispanic,* the advertising director reports directly to the publisher, emphasizing the importance of the position.

Selling advertising is one of the most challenging jobs in publishing. It involves intelligence and knowledge of both the magazine and the advertiser. It requires spunk and energy. Romeo Perez says that when recruiting

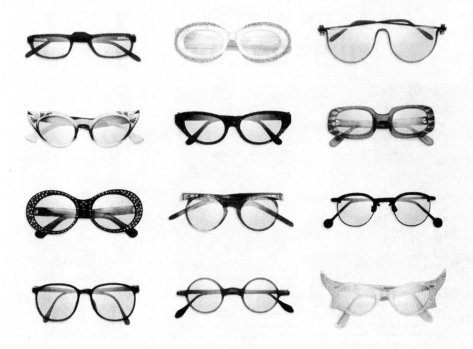

It takes a lot of different points of view to come up with one grand vision.

Though values in the world and the work place may change over time, the values that Hyatt lives by have never waivered. We believe that regardless of background, we can always learn from each other. And we believe that, when you offer talented people unlimited respect and opportunities, your company's success and vision will be unlimited, too.

potential staff members, he looks for people who have any type of sales experience and are exceptionally organized. While it is important for sales representatives to understand the Hispanic market, culture, and people, they need not be of Hispanic descent. Salespeople have to be able to listen to their clients and understand their business. It is for this reason that publications spend a great deal of time recruiting and training their sales staff.

About 50 percent of *Hispanic*'s ads are for products, especially automobiles. Some of *Hispanic*'s ads for cigarettes and alcohol have been criticized by the Hispanic community. Many people point to the high incidence of lung cancer and alcohol-related disease in the Hispanic community and believe that a magazine that claims to support Hispanics shouldn't allow these companies access to its publication.

But Alfredo Estrada says alcohol and cigarette ads account for a very small percentage of product advertising sales. "Generally our magazine targets college-educated people in their thirties who can make informed decisions on their own," he says, expressing weariness with the issue. "You can decide to look at our magazine if you want to and not look at it if you don't want. We're not forcing our publication on people." He explains that the issues distributed in the schools are directed to teachers and principals and that they control distribution to the students.

Almost 25 percent of *Hispanic*'s ads are placed by companies looking to recruit Hispanics. Many employers would like to vary the ethnic makeup of their staffs. Some, such as the Federal Bureau of Investigation, the Department of Justice, and the U.S. Foreign Service, are under government orders to do so. Marketing director Tony Barajas says these clients want to reach a nationwide group of possible employees and see *Hispanic* magazine as one of the few publications that can deliver the audience they want.

Another 18 percent of the ads in *Hispanic* are placed by companies eager to highlight their diversity. These are called corporate image advertisements and feature Hispanics, usually executive and other top-level workers, who are employed at these companies.

The rest of the sales come from advertisers pushing minority business development opportunities.

While it is important for a magazine to have good circulation figures

Romeo and Laura Figueroa—advertising and marketing—often work together to promote the magazine.

(the number of copies purchased or distributed), it is equally important to have readers with good *demographics*. This term refers to the characteristics of the readers, such as their age and how much money they make. Advertisers are looking to reach the people who are most likely to buy their product. The owners of Rolls Royce, Ltd., would rather not advertise their automobiles in the high-circulation *People* magazine since most of that publication's readers could not afford the car. The owners might look to a lower-circulation magazine, such as the *New York Times Sunday Magazine,* which attracts readers with a higher income than those of *People.* On the other hand, the makers of a popular lower-priced automobile might advertise in *People* knowing that most of its readers could afford their car.

Hispanic completes a national reader survey every several years, with smaller surveys conducted almost every year. Such surveys reveal important information such as income and education level of the magazine's readers, as well as their buying habits (for example, how often these readers buy cars).

Research shows that *Hispanic*'s readers are family oriented, the majority are between the ages of eighteen and forty-four, most have attended or graduated from college, and almost 65 percent were born in the United States. They are also high wage earners. This young, upscale, college-educated readership is eagerly sought by advertisers, especially corporate, financial, and recruitment companies. The "Latinos on the Info Superhighway" story helped to attract more of those readers. Keeping a pulse on his readership is the most important of Tony Barajas's many jobs. These demographics allow *Hispanic* to sell an average of forty-five ads a month and sometimes up to eighty. The magazine is never at a loss to fill ad space.

But despite its reader and client acceptance, *Hispanic* magazine suffers from the same unexpected problem that eventually hurt *Vista* magazine. Publishers of both magazines say that their biggest hurdle to making money has been getting Hispanic advertising agencies to buy ads in their publications. Arturo Villar and Alfredo Estrada both proclaim that many of these agencies, used by large corporations to buy advertising that will reach Hispanics, have convinced their clients that the only way to reach this ethnic group is through the Spanish-language medium. "There is a lot of resistance from these agencies," says Alfredo. "For years they've told their clients that the agencies could be effective for them if they bought advertising in Spanish-language publications. Now we're telling them English-language can be effective too."

Public relations director Randy Belcher-Torres is another staff member who works tirelessly to generate interest in *Hispanic* magazine. By creating interest in his or her publication, a good public relations specialist can help increase circulation and advertising sales, and create goodwill in the community. Randy handles press, corporate, and government relations. He spends much of his time making presentations to school groups, major Hispanic organizations, and journalism groups, who enjoy his upbeat manner.

Along with Tony Barajas, Randy acts as the main contact for anyone looking to find out information about *Hispanic* magazine. "Tony and I are basically the communicators of the magazine," says Randy, a fifth-generation New Mexican whose ancestors tilled the land before it was a state. "My job is to get to as many people as possible and communicate to them the benefits of our magazine. A PR person has to be intensely involved in the product or business."

Gloria Baragan, a teacher in a poor El Paso, Texas school district, was one of the first readers to reveal to Randy just how special his new magazine could be to the Hispanic community. She walked into *Hispanic*'s office one day in 1988 and inquired whether her class could be sent several copies of the three-month-old publication. Randy had recently sent several thousand copies to educators around the country, which was how Gloria Baragan had

As an account executive, Robert Morin convinces advertisers that Hispanic *has the readers they want to reach.*

ANNUAL SALARIES OF MAGAZINE PERSONNEL

Salaries vary according to the publication's circulation size, the region of the country where it is based, and the age and sex of the employee (according to an annual survey of salaries by *Folio: The Magazine for Magazine Management*). There are other variables that also have an impact on salaries, including type of magazine—trade, consumer, or business—or type of circulation—paid or unpaid.

Generally, magazines that are based in the Northeast pay more than those in the South (where *Hispanic* is based), magazines with larger circulations pay more than smaller ones, and men make more than women in similar positions. For example, the average annual salary for a male art director at a consumer magazine is $40,582, whereas that for a female is only $35,063.

The annual salaries that follow are based on a survey of magazine professionals conducted in the spring of 1994. The listing includes title of job and brief description, the salary range reported by those surveyed, and the average salary for an employee of a consumer magazine with a circulation between 100,000 and 499,999.

Position	Salary range	Average salary at consumer magazine
Editor-in-chief Sets editorial policy. Might be in charge of other departments, including sales.	$10,000 to $400,000	$70,705
Executive editor Responsible for editorial direction and content.	$13,080 to $443,000	$48,022

Managing editor Coordinates the editorial departments to ensure that the magazine is published on time.	$21,500 to $210,000	$36,496
Senior editor Plans and writes features and other articles.	$17,500 to $76,000	$41,091
Art director Oversees art department.	$16,000 to $115,000	$39,470
Associate art director Assists with the design and layout of the magazine.	$20,500 to $56,000	$38,000
Ad sales director The top ad sales manager. Sets policy, hires sales force and trains personnel.	$16,000 to $200,000	$107,725
Ad sales manager Manages day-to-day sales programs.	$3,500 to $111,000	$70,000
Account executive Maintains and develops accounts and makes sales calls.	$5,000 to $145,000	$58,079

Circulation director	$16,000 to $180,000	$56,206

The top circulation executive. Coordinates circulation marketing efforts and trains personnel.

Many members of the advertising staff receive sales bonuses and commissions in addition to their salaries.

first seen the magazine. But she taught children in elementary school, a group the owners of *Hispanic* had considered too young for their magazine.

"She talked about early intervention and the need for role models," remembers Randy. "And she was very adamant that the magazine could be effective. She made a lot of the same arguments we were making about the magazine." Soon after agreeing to send the next issue, Randy visited Gloria Baragan's school district to give presentations to principals, teachers, and students in various grades. In one second-grade class, a young girl came over and requested a magazine, which featured singer Linda Ronstadt on the cover. "This interest among students and teachers did not show up in our marketing surveys," notes Randy.

The experience with Gloria Baragan's school district encouraged *Hispanic* magazine to create AHEAD (America's Hispanic Education Achievement Drive), which provides magazines to schools. Another program distributes magazines to over 100 colleges around the country. These programs hope to build self-esteem among young Hispanics, at the same time offering teachers much needed additional class material. It was a match made in heaven, says publisher Alfredo Estrada.

"Our marketing plan from the beginning was to serve as communicators of positive role models for Hispanics," Alfredo says. "The whole idea behind the magazine was to take advantage of what we considered a solid business opportunity while filling a void in the coverage of our community."

As circulation manager, Rochelle Herrera, can attest, there's no point in publishing a magazine if it's not out there being read.

· 7 ·

Getting the Publication Out There

Publishers do not create publications to display them on their bookshelves. Circulation and distribution are the final and most important steps in the publishing process. Magazines must establish a six-month record of distribution in order to determine what the magazine will charge for its advertising space. In January 1995, *Hispanic*'s circulation stood at 250,000. This number paled in comparison to the figures for much larger publications like *Essence* (850,000 issues), which itself is dwarfed by *People* (3.2 million) and *Time* (4.3 million). It is particularly important for *Hispanic* to have steady circulation numbers because many of the issues are distributed free.

Magazines circulate through subscription, single-copy sales, and controlled circulation. Subscriptions, which are contracts between the reader and publisher to deliver the publication, bring in less money because they are usually discounted from the single-copy price. But since the money is received in advance of delivering all the issues, it can be used for production. *Hispanic* sells 40,000 copies a month through subscription agreements.

Readers who buy the magazine from a newsstand pay a higher price for single copies but are more important to advertisers because by buying the publication they usually have a higher probability of reading it. For these magazines, the cover story and design must stand out in order to compete with the hundreds of other publications on the newsstands.

"The magazine cover is not as important a selling tool for us because we don't sell many magazines on the newsstand," says circulation director Gary

Circulation director Gary Meo has to keep people ordering—and paying for—Hispanic.

Meo. *Hispanic* sells roughly 4,000 copies at newsstands. "But I do look at the cover story to spot potential markets. If I get a cover story on education, I do some extra promotions with colleges and schools."

As noted earlier, *Hispanic* magazine is mostly distributed through a controlled-circulation system. Controlled circulation magazines distribute their issues for free to a very select group of readers whose names are from credit card companies and other businesses. Airline magazines and theater programs are examples of controlled circulation publications. Advertisers pay a premium for knowing that specific kinds of readers will be exposed to their ads. Usually these readers are influential people or individuals who can promote the magazine through word of mouth, such as journalists, government officials, or teachers. It is the circulation director's job to strike a balance between subscriptions, single-copy sales, controlled circulation issues, and direct promotion costs. An independent company called the Business Publi-

GARY MEO

Circulation director Gary Meo is a journalist who tasted the business side of publishing and never went back. This thirty-six-year-old New York native always wanted to be a journalist. He attended the State University at Binghamton, where he worked at the college radio station and wrote newscasts. Then he entered New York University's prestigious journalism program. "I worked on the magazine and college newspaper, and I was sure that life was for me," Gary remembers.

After graduating and sending out more than 200 resumes, however, he found that no one was hiring. "I got involved with magazine marketing and found it very fast-paced and exciting. [I did] . . . better than some of my friends from school, who ended up at small newspapers in middle America."

In 1985, Gary moved to California to become the marketing manager for the *Los Angeles Times*. He stayed eight years. By 1993, he was tired of leading such a hectic life. "My wife was born in Austin, and we just needed a break from the big-city life. Austin is more laid back than . . . L.A.," he says. When *Hispanic* decided to move to Austin, a friend introduced him to the publisher, Alfredo Estrada.

Circulation directors are responsible for getting new readers and keeping current readers satisfied. Because of the importance of getting the magazine out, many times a circulation director can advance to associate publisher or even publisher.

"I had never been a magazine circulation professional, but I knew many sides of the business," Gary says. "Alfredo has invested a lot of time creating relationships with professional Hispanic organizations, and it has paid off. That relationship has made it easy for me."

cations of America (BPA) checks the accuracy of *Hispanic*'s claimed paid circulation.

A magazine's circulation department is often described as a business unto itself. The circulation staff must deal with customers, keep track of buying behavior, participate in marketing, and produce and write a large number of promotional materials. Getting people to renew subscriptions might be the most important of Gary Meo's jobs. *Hispanic* magazine's renewal rate hovers around 30 percent, a bit below average for a consumer magazine, according to Gary. "One of my major concerns this year," he says, "is to increase that rate." But the staff takes pride in the fact that of every 100 people who order the magazine and are billed, almost 65 end up paying for the subscription, a high rate in the industry.

Gary uses different techniques and outside agencies to help distribute *Hispanic* magazine. Subscription agencies, the gigantic Publishers Clearing House being the largest, are companies that distribute the magazine, taking a cut of the subscription price as payment. Other agencies specialize in getting the magazine to libraries or to readers door-to-door. The school and college giveaway programs (discussed in chapter 6) were first used by the Johnson Publishing Company, publishers of *Ebony* and *Jet*, two of the biggest African-American magazines on the market. These programs look to promote positive role models among youngsters while trying to create potential subscribers.

"I remember one of the big measuring sticks to being a grown-up was when you got a free *Jet* in your own apartment," says *Hispanic*'s former circulation manager Brian Maye, who once supervised AHEAD. "These programs don't make much money, but they do create loyal readers." Gary Meo says that the programs also help boost the image of the magazine among educators and future educated readers.

Hispanic magazine's subscribers receive the publication through the mail directly from the printer in Florida, while large bulk deliveries to one location are shipped by truck. Almost one-third of each month's issues are distributed in Texas, one-third in California, and the final third throughout the rest of the country. The hope is that only a few copies wind up in storage back at the home office in Austin, Texas.

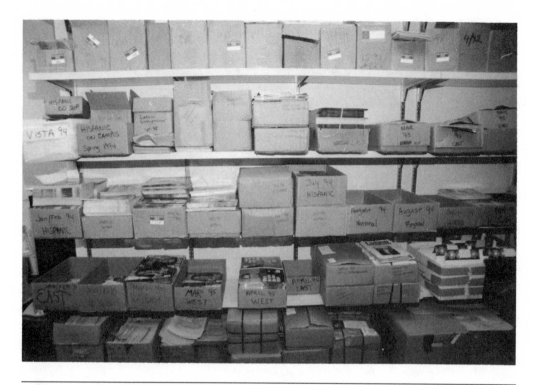

There are not many issues left of each month's Hispanic—*a relief to circulation and marketing people.*

"It's a good feeling to get the magazine out and then stumble across it at a doctor's office or a library," notes Gary. "We realize a dream here in that we do no promotion on TV or radio and we get letters every day asking for subscriptions. So I'd say we're touching something in people."

Alfredo Estrada has studied the magazines of other minority groups and knows that Hispanic *has the potential for great success.*

· 8 ·

The Future Is Now

The "Latinos on the Info Superhighway" story identified the road on which the Hispanic Publishing Corporation wants to travel. It is a road to the future that will allow publishers to send their publications out through computers and phone wires. "We recognize that the way the media are being delivered is going through a revolution right now," says Alfredo Estrada. "Being part of that revolution is good business."

Fred and Alfredo Estrada already view the Hispanic Publishing Corporation as a good business opportunity that serves a positive purpose in their culture and community. The company now circulates an average of 1.3 million copies of its publications each month to various communities around the country.

But Alfredo Estrada says that despite the success of his publications and his competitors, there is much room for growth in the Hispanic publishing market. Getting *Hispanic* on-line so that subscribers can access the publication through their computers could lead to services that would offer stories, advertising, help-wanted ads, research, or other products important to Hispanics. And some major media companies are also starting to see the possibilities in the Hispanic market.

To better target the growing Hispanic population in California, the *Los Angeles Times* has started a separate Spanish-language publication that is inserted inside the main newspaper. The *New York Daily News* has added a Spanish-language edition for its Hispanic readers, while Time Warner, Inc., a onetime investor in *Vista* magazine, is planning several Hispanic-targeted

Coast to Coast

Taking a Jab at Illiteracy

Julio Cesar Chavez knows what it feels like to struggle. The legendary boxer was one of ten siblings who grew up in a railroad car, provided by his father's employer, in Culiacan, Mexico. It was not hard to find inspiration there, however. His father Rodolfo, a train conductor, once saved an entire village by heroically jumping onto a burning runaway train and stopping it.

The World Champion boxer Chavez, now a millionaire, is using his success to inspire others. This time his opponent is not a Super Lightweight fighter but a heavyweight problem—illiteracy. Chavez has joined forces with Coors Brewing Company in its ongoing literacy campaign. He will make personal appearances in predominantly Hispanic communities in Texas and California, and his face will grace posters promoting the program "Leyendo, Que Bien Se Pasa."

An estimated 56 percent of adult Hispanics in the United States are functionally illiterate. It's about time we find strategies to knock out this problem. For more information, call the Coors Literacy Hotline at (800) 626-4601.

Eunice Moscoso

Environmentalists Cross the Line

They work opposite ends of the fence, and sometimes from different philosophies. But against the backdrop of NAFTA, U.S. and Mexican environmental groups are enjoying unprecedented cross-border cooperation.

"NAFTA opened a window of opportunity for both sides to work together politically, to articulate problems and solu-

tions," says Irasema Coronado, a researcher with El Colegio de la Frontera Norte in Nogales, Sonora, and a member of the Binational Health and Environmental Coalition.

Known as "La Red," for "network," the international coalition embraces approximately 50 smaller affiliations, all focusing on the border's massive pollution problems. La Red acts as a conduit for transferring information between Mexican and U.S. environmental groups. It regularly provides U.S. groups with insight into Mexico's political scene. In return, U.S. activists help La Red gain access to policymakers here.

"We now have a direct line on information from Mexico, which is otherwise very difficult to come by," says Geoffrey Land, border coordinator of the Arizona-based Border Ecology Project, a La Red affiliate. "Together, we take that information and mold it into binational realities."

The relationship isn't hassle-free, however. Mexicans can have their patriotism questioned when it is perceived that they work too closely with "gringos." And U.S. environmentalists, accustomed to high-tech communication, often hit snags south of the border. "There isn't much Internet or e-mail down here," says Coronado. "Most Mexicans don't even have computers."

Still, just like contaminated water and dirty air, common goals transcend national boundaries. Groups like La Red realize that a cleaner planet benefits us all.

Tim Vanderpool

Danza Borinqueña

Serious dancers begin practicing their art at a young age, dreaming of the day when they might appear onstage as part of a dance company. But not Rochester, New York's, Nydia Padilla-Rodriguez.

Padilla-Rodriguez, who began studying dance at thirteen, was invited to join Garth Fagan's renowned Bottom-of-the-Bucket Dance Company after only three years of training. But shortly after achieving her goal, she found herself facing a decision between life in the spotlight and college.

Luckily for Rochester's young people, Padilla-Rodriguez chose college, earning a bachelor's in dance and elementary education and a master's in education

Padilla-Rodriguez (top left) lines up with her Borinquen Dance Theatre girls.

from SUNY Brockport. She has since built a career around teaching Caribbean dance and has created her own company, named the Borinquen Dance Theatre (in honor of the indigenous name for Puerto Rico). Borinquen, the Ensemble-in-Residence at the Hochstein Music School in Rochester, is comprised of ethnically diverse dancers, ages 14 to 22, as well as a children's group, who perform throughout the Northeast.

Curiously, the company focusing on the African, Taino Indian, and Spanish influences of Puerto Rican culture started out as an adult exercise class which evolved into a performing arts group. But while working with adults, Padilla-Rodriguez said, "I began to think about all of the problems that youth are having." She changed the focus of the group to work with adoles-

NO MORE STATUS QUO!

A nationwide survey found that 54% of Hispanics want a third political party.

SOURCE: TIMES MIRROR CENTER FOR PEOPLE & THE PRESS. SEPTEMBER 1994.

publications. These companies are finally recognizing the estimated $200 billion of buying power in the Hispanic community.

In making a case for the potential of Hispanic publications, Alfredo Estrada points to the phenomenal success of African-American magazines: There is not only the 1.8-million-circulation *Ebony*, which is a general-interest magazine like *Hispanic*, but *Essence* (for women), *Black Enterprise* (for business owners), and *African-American Heritage* (about the black American experience). "Those [black-owned publications] are the best examples for us to see that there is a market," Alfredo says. "Hispanics are going to be the largest minority group in the next twenty-five years, so we will have the potential readers."

But many of the African-American publications have been around for years and have collected much support among African-American advertising agencies and a wide range of corporations. Hispanic publications, however, still have to overcome the confusion over what language is most effective in meeting the needs of the Hispanic community. This issue is cited by most publishers as the single most important decision in planning a Hispanic publication.

"There is a lot of confusion about what language to publish in, and that remains our biggest problem," says Fred Estrada. "But it depends on your magazine's target. Our audience for *Vista* is bilingual. Our audience for *Hispanic* is mostly English speaking."

The Hispanic Publishing Corporation doesn't seem to be paying attention to any confusion or lack of support from Hispanic advertising agencies. *Hispanic* magazine now publishes a healthy forty to sixty ads a month. And a January–February double issue in 1995 contained 80 pages of ads.

In its seventh year of existence, there are enough projects to keep *Hispanic* staff members busy into the next century. "Our number-one priority is to expand the franchise we have with *Hispanic* magazine," says Alfredo Estrada. "Music magazines, publications that target young teens, women's publications are also things we are considering. I think we've proven that we have a voice to offer."

Glossary

art director—the person in charge of designing and controlling how the publication looks.

bilingual—communicating in or being able to use two languages.

byline—the writer's name, usually found at the beginning of the story.

caption—a short description of a photo or other illustration, usually found next to or under the piece of art.

consumer magazine—a publication that offers its readers articles on a variety of subjects, such as life in general, sports, education, and entertainment.

controlled circulation—a distribution system that allows people to get the magazine for free if they meet specific qualifications.

copy editor—an expert in grammar, usage, and style who corrects the stories submitted by writers.

demographics—the statistical study of human populations, including such characteristics as age and income.

design—the arrangement of the parts or details of a publication.

distributors—the people in charge of getting a publication to its readers.

editor—a person who supervises the publication of printed material.

fact checker—a person who checks all the facts in a story.

feature—a long, in-depth story.

film—a negative produced from a photograph of the completed pages.

freelancer—a person, especially a writer, artist, or musician, who does not work for one employer only but who sells his or her services to several employers as those services are needed.

halftone—a photograph or drawing that has been converted into a pattern of tiny dots. By screening images this way, printing presses are able to reproduce shades of gray.

headlines—large type running above a story to summarize its content and attract the reader's attention.

infographic—computer generated graphics that give readers a variety of information through words as well as visuals, presenting complicated material in an easy-to-digest form.

layout—the placement of text and art on a page.

logo—the design or symbol that identifies a company or group.

loupe—a small magnifying glass.

managing editor—the person who supervises the day-to-day operations of a publication.

manuscript—typewritten or handwritten version of a book or other work.

marketing—methods and activities employed to promote a favorable impression with the public.

marketing director—person who supervises all the marketing of a company.

market study—a study of readers used to sell the publication to certain advertisers.

nameplate—the name of the magazine as it's displayed on page one.

page proof—a test page produced for a final edit before the page gets printed.

pagination—the process of creating a page on a computer.

press run—the printing of the publication.

preview issue—the first issue of a publication, usually used as a test to see if readers and advertisers like it.

production—the process of producing printed material.

production manager—the person who supervises the different steps in producing a publication.

proofreader—a person who reads and marks corrections, typically on a set of page proofs.

publisher—the person who oversees and is responsible for the entire operation of a publishing company.

query—a short outline sent by a writer to an editor detailing ideas for a story he or she wants to write.

rate card—a sheet containing a breakdown of prices charged for advertising in a publication. The larger the ad, the higher the price.

separation house—a company that produces copy in terms of three colors (plus black) used in printing a photograph, illustration, or page.

sidebar—a brief story with a special angle that goes with the main story.

story budget—a list of stories to be published.

typeface—all type of a particular design.

typography—the arrangement and appearance of words and text.

For More Information

Association of Hispanic Arts
173 East 116 Street
New York, NY 10029
(212) 860-5445

Association of Latin Americans
   in Communications
P.O. Box 785
Natik, MA 01760
(508) 975-2704

California Chicano News Media Association
School of Journalism
University of Southern California
Los Angeles, CA 90089
(213) 743-7158

Chicago Association of Hispanic Journalists
WGN Radio
3114 West Palmer Square
Chicago, IL 60611

Colorado Hispanic Media Association
2525 Sixteenth Street, #214
Denver, CO 80201
(303) 458-8960

Concerned Media Professionals
220 West Sixth Street
Tucson, AZ 85702
(602) 884-3743

Florida Association of Hispanic Journalists
P.O. Box 172154
Hialeah, FL 33017
(305) 599-5302 or (305) 599-5318

Hispanic Academy of Media Arts & Sciences
P.O. Box 1476
Burbank, CA 91507
(818) 954-2720

Hispanic Journalists of Central Arizona
P.O. Box 1950
Phoenix, AZ 85001
(602) 271-8222

Hispanic News Media Association
1420 N. Street, NW
Washington, DC 21005
(202) 234-0280

Latinos in Communications
110 Pacific Avenue, Suite 150
San Francisco, CA 94111
(415) 979-4168

National Association of Hispanic Journalists
National Press Building, Suite 1193
Washington, DC 20045
(202) 662-7147

National Association of Hispanic Publications
310 South Frio Street, Suite 105
San Antonio, TX 78207
(512) 270-1290

National Hispanic Media Coalition
5400 East Olympic Boulevard, No. 250
Los Angeles, CA 90022

New Mexico Minority Media Association
P.O. Box 1351
Albuquerque, NM 87103

Puerto Rican Journalists Association
P.O. Box 4187
San Juan, PR 00936

San Antonio Association of Hispanic Journalists
P.O. Box 2171
San Antonio, TX 78297
(512) 255-7411

For Further Reading

Click, J. W. *Magazine Editing and Production*. Dubuque, Iowa: W. C. Brown, 1990.

Gunderloy, Mike. *The World of Zines: A Guide to the Independent Magazine Revolution*. New York: Penguin Books, 1992.

Jaspersohn, William. *Magazine: Behind the Scenes at Sports Illustrated*. Boston: Little, Brown, 1983.

Magazines Career Directory. Hawthorne, N.J.: Career Press, 1987.

Mogel, Leonard. *The Magazine: Everything You Need to Know to Make It in the Magazine Business*. Englewood Cliffs, N.J.: Prentice-Hall, 1979.

Pattis, S. William. *Opportunities in Magazine Publishing Careers*. Lincolnwood, Ill.: VGM Career Horizons, 1992.

Williams, W. P. *How to Start Your Own Magazine*. Chicago: Contemporary Books, 1978.

Index